25 DAILY DEVOTIONS FOR ADVENT & CHRISTMAS

MARGARET FEINBERG

 Some of the research and content based on and taken directly from the sermons taught by Troy Champ at Capital Church. Used with permission.

Celebrate
Wonder & Joy

A Letter from Margaret

Sweet Friend,

If you're like me, the weeks before Christmas overflow with lists and to-dos. Instead of living in wild expectation of Jesus' birth, I find myself in lines at grocery stores, boutiques, and big box stores.

Yet Advent beckons us to prepare for the arrival of a tiny infant with a frame so small you could cradle Him in the palms of your hands.

Advent comes from the Latin word *adventus* which means "coming." The purpose of Advent is two-fold: a celebration of the arrival of Christ and an anticipation of Christ's return.

Advent awakens our senses to the "now" and "not yet" as God's children.
Advent alerts our hearts to God's work in the waiting.
Advent amplifies our awareness of the our need for a Savior.

Celebrate Wonder and Joy provides 25 Scripture readings coupled with a devotional entry and reflection questions. I'm indebted to the research and insights from my pastor, Troy Champ at Capital Church, for his insights during the development of this study.

You're invited to gather around the table. Invite a friend, your kids, or grandkids to join. Grab a handful of colored pencils, markers, or crayons to slow down as you read the Scripture. Take time to circle the verbs, underline the names, and consider the details of the text as you doodle, color, and reflect.

Please don't keep what you are learning to yourself. Share what you are discovering on Facebook, Twitter, Instagram, or your blog using the hashtag: #CelebrateWonder. Join our community—there's plenty of room for you.

My prayer is that during this time you'll step back from the hustle and bustle of the holidays and make room for Him.

Much love and Merry Christmas,

Margaret, Leif, and Hershey

How to use the Color Method

Creativity splashes through the readings of Scripture. I'm learning to let my inner doodler dance and play. I scribble like a 4-year-old, but the swirls and colors provide time for the words and the phrases to sink deeper into my soul. I hope they will for you, too.

Coloring slows our pace.
Coloring highlights the patterns, repeated words, and holy emphasis.
Coloring invites us beyond reading the Scripture and invites the Scripture to read us.

The readings in *Celebrate Wonder and Joy* are short. The Color Method will add a few minutes as you read through each portion of Scripture several times. The depth, the richness, and the discoveries make this extra effort worth every moment.

Here are possibilities for different colors:

- Circle verbs in **red** to highlight the activity of God and people.
- Circle places in **brown** to note location.
- Circle names in **purple** to identify people.
- Mark numbers in **orange** to identify numerals, which may have Biblical significance.
- Mark the Holy Spirit, angels, and the prophetic in **blue** to identify God's presence and handiwork.
- Scribble observations in **green** to record insights.

Feel free to choose your favorite hues.

Following the Scripture reading, you'll find a devotional that zeroes in on one concept from the passage. I wrote these to spur your thoughts and hearts Christward. Each reading closes with reflection questions designed for personal or small group use.

As you finish studying each day, consider how to respond in an active way. You may be nudged to prayer, repentance, a generous act, or a kind word. Ask God how to be both a hearer and a doer of the day's reading.

DAY ONE
HARK! WHEN YOU HEAR THE BELLS
ISAIAH 7:14 NASB

14 Therefore the Lord Himself will give you a sign: Behold, a virgin will be with child and bear a son, and she will call His name Immanuel.

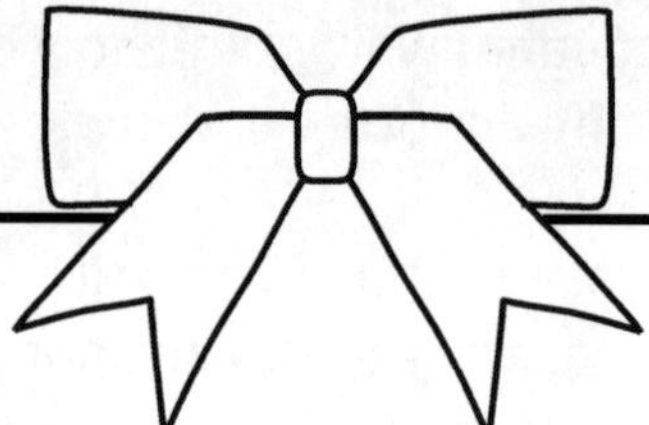

If you thumb through Scripture, you'll notice how waiting weaves itself into the fabric of history. God waits. Creation waits. Humankind waits. We wait for reconciliation and redemption, healing and wholeness. We crane our necks, strain our ears for bells of freedom to ring and jingle.

Throughout the Bible, a question reverberates:

"How long?"

Those two little words appear more than fifty times in Scripture, and it's no wonder, because waiting is part of all our stories. Adam and Eve wait, fresh fruit staining their faces, for God to discover what they have done. Noah waits for the first raindrops to pitter-patter on his odd-shaped boat. Abram waits for a promised son, Jacob waits for a promised wife, and the Israelites wait for a promised new life.

For four hundred years, the prophets wait in silence for a syllable from God. All heaven and humanity hold their breath for the arrival of Immanuel.

Deep in the fabric of our souls, we wonder, "How long must we wait?"

The truth about waiting is God asks this question, too.

In Exodus 10:3, Moses and Aaron deliver God's message to Pharaoh: "This is what the Lord, the God of the Hebrews, says: 'How long will you refuse to humble yourself before Me? Let My people go, that they may serve Me.'"

God is at work in the waiting, even when the wait seems long, to bring the Israelites and each of us, step by step, toward salvation and redemption.

God sends a baby boy in a basket to deliver the Israelites freedom.

God sends a baby boy in a barn to deliver us freedom.

God asks, "How long?" then delivers the answer, the gift of freedom, in person.

Hark! The bells of freedom in Christ ring for you.

Your freedom arrives in a divine plan, a holy person, a sacred child. Whenever you hear bells jingle this holiday season, celebrate the wonder that your freedom rings in Christ.

Reflection Questions:

1. What are you waiting on God for most this Advent season?
2. In what area of your life do you need to hear Christ ring the bells of freedom?
3. How do materialism and commercialism drown out the bells of freedom Christ has rung for you?
4. Using the Color Method, what stood out to you most from today's Scripture?
5. What do you find most challenging in today's passage? Most comforting?

DAY TWO

GOD IS NOT AFRAID OF THIS

MATTHEW 1:1-7 NKJV

1 The book of the genealogy of Jesus Christ, the Son of David, the Son of Abraham: 2 Abraham
begot Isaac, Isaac begot Jacob, and Jacob begot Judah and his brothers. 3 Judah begot Perez
and Zerah by Tamar, Perez begot Hezron, and Hezron begot Ram. 4 Ram begot Amminadab,
Amminadab begot Nahshon, and Nahshon begot Salmon. 5 Salmon begot Boaz by Rahab, Boaz
begot Obed by Ruth, Obed begot Jesse, 6 and Jesse begot David the king. David the king begot
Solomon by her who had been the wife of Uriah. 7 Solomon begot Rehoboam, Rehoboam begot
Abijah, and Abijah begot Asa.

Matthew launches his story with a genealogy of Jesus, marking the beginning of the arrival of the Messiah and the coming of the kingdom of God. Several women appear in the genealogy—a rarity in Jewish genealogical records. To the first readers of Matthew's Gospel, their inclusion caused jaws to drop and mouths to gape.

These women hang dirty laundry on Jesus' family tree. Tamar is abandoned and pretends to be a prostitute. Rahab is a prostitute and traitor; Ruth, a gentile widow and immigrant; Bathsheba, an adulteress.

For the Biblical statistician, three of the four were gentiles, considered unclean by the Jews, and three of the four were involved in adultery. Those are bad odds.

Yet Matthew does more than mention these women, he highlights them, and in the process, reveals that God uses people with shady pasts to unfold His plan to save the world. Gentiles. Sinners. Prostitutes. Adulteresses. And men who deceive, murder, and steal. Together, their stories remind us:

God uses imperfect people to accomplish His perfect purposes.

These women and men are vital to delivering the Greatest Gift to the world.

Like each of them, none of your past sins keep you from service in God's plan. No matter where you've been, no matter what you've done, God wants you to be part of His redemptive work.

Reflection Questions:

1. Do you see anything in yourself in the imperfect people in this genealogy?
2. Where have you disqualified yourself from being used by God? How has God used you anyway?
3. How have you seen God use broken, imperfect people in your life?
4. Using the Color Method, what stood out to you most from today's Scripture?
5. What do you find most challenging in today's lesson? What do you find most comforting?

DAY THREE
THIS IMPORTANT NUMBER WILL SURPRISE YOU
MATTHEW 1:16-17 NKJV

16 And Jacob begot Joseph the husband of Mary, of whom was born Jesus who is called
Christ. 17 So all the generations from Abraham to David are fourteen generations, from David
until the captivity in Babylon are fourteen generations, and from the captivity in Babylon
until the Christ are fourteen generations.

Biblical genealogies tempt us to skim in a mad dash to get to the next section of Scripture. Yet Matthew packs his genealogy with rich information and theology.

If you squint at the names, you'll discover one mentioned more than the others: David.

Now Hebrews used their letters as numbers. David's name includes three consonants and a numerical value of 14. Matthew lists David's name as No. 14.

Reflecting on the genealogy, Matthew lists three 14-generation periods. From Abraham to David, Israel expands. From David until captivity, the kingdom contracts. Fourteen generations later, one who is called the Son of David appears. The number 14 matters because Matthew uses this number, which is two times seven (this divine number symbolizes perfection), to show God working throughout the ages.

Jesus' messianic title as the Son of David reveals Christ as the long-awaited Savior and Deliverer of the world. David is promised that one of his offspring will rule forever (2 Samuel 7:12-16). God fulfills His word by sending His Word at the precise time (John 1:1-18).

God's people waited through famine, slavery, terrible kings, exile, and Roman oppression for centuries. Though God's timing is rarely our timing, rest assured:

God is always on time.

The miracle of the Incarnation is grace and truth. Grace because God comes to our rescue. Truth because God keeps His promises made through the eons and dwells with us in the person of Christ, who is fully God and fully human. What joy we find in knowing that God's timing is always perfect.

Reflection Questions:

1. When are you most tempted to doubt God's timing?
2. What are you most tired of waiting for in your life?
3. Describe a moment when God worked with wondrous timing in your life.
4. Using the Color Method, what stood out to you most from today's Scripture?
5. What do you find most challenging in today's devotional? Most comforting?

DAY FOUR
WHEN YOU DON'T KNOW HOW YOUR STORY WILL END
LUKE 1:13-15 KJV

13 But the angel said unto him, Fear not, Zacharias: for thy prayer is heard; and thy wife
Elisabeth shall bear thee a son, and thou shalt call his name John.
14 And thou shalt have joy and gladness; and many shall rejoice at his birth.
15 For he shall be great in the sight of the Lord, and shall drink neither wine nor strong drink;
and he shall be filled with the Holy Ghost, even from his mother's womb.

Sometimes it feels like so much of our lives is spent waiting. Waiting to graduate. Waiting to land a job. Waiting to meet the one. Waiting to become pregnant. Waiting for an empty nest. Waiting for retirement. Waiting for different circumstances. Waiting for a breakthrough.

We drum our fingers. Twiddle our thumbs. Play with our hair. Pace. Or if you're like me, make that loud exhaling sound. *Hummmhhhh.*

Maybe waiting comes easy for you. For me, waiting is hard, downright brutal.

Yet waiting doesn't have to be a waste—especially when we learn to wait well.

Elizabeth and Zechariah spent their youth waiting for a baby. In ancient culture, childlessness carried a heavy stigma that brought deep shame. Some rabbis taught that infertility was evidence of divine disfavor. This couple ages and their hope of a child fades with each passing year.

Then Zechariah receives the once-in-a-lifetime honor to burn incense in the Holy of Holies inside of the temple. Once inside, Zechariah encounters an angel who tells him his prayers have been heard. The couple will have the longed-for child, the forerunner of the Messiah.

We celebrate with Elizabeth and Zachariah because we know how their story ends. But often, we don't know how our story ends.

Waiting may cause us to doubt the goodness of God. Like me, you too may become impatient, graspy, grumpypants. You may try to take matters into your own hands or rush the process. Like Elizabeth and Zachariah, remember:

God is worth and worthy of the wait.

Even when Elizabeth and Zechariah didn't see God moving, they continued to live lives that were righteous, blameless, above reproach. They continued to wait on God, because He is worth the wait and worthy of the wait. Even when God does not produce that which we wait on, faithfulness expresses adoration for God.

Isaiah 64:4 says, "Since ancient times no one has heard, no ear has perceived, no eye has seen any God besides you, who acts on behalf of those who wait for him."

God does not call you to wait alone, but rather to wait on Him alone.

This holiday season make sure you don't become so focused on what you're waiting on that you miss the celebration of the One worthy of the wait.

Reflection Questions:

1. Make a list of three areas of waiting in your life. Find a Scripture to circle around each area in prayer.
2. In each, are you more tempted to wait on circumstances to change or on God?
3. How do you suspect that God is stretching you through waiting?
4. Using the Color Method, what stood out to you most from today's Scripture?
5. What do you find most challenging in today's reading about waiting?

DAY FIVE
WHAT TO DO WHEN LIFE GETS COMPLICATED
LUKE 1:26-27 NIV

26 In the sixth month of Elizabeth's pregnancy, God sent the angel Gabriel to Nazareth, a
town in Galilee, 27 to a virgin pledged to be married to a man named Joseph, a descendant of
David. The virgin's name was Mary.

Gabriel's first announcement comes to a priest at the high point of his career, in a public act of worship, in God's Holy City.

This announcement comes to a young girl from the boonies.

Oh, how the world anticipates a Savior—one who will announce peace and deliverance, breathtaking news. The world vibrates with centuries of expectation.

Mary, too.

She knows the Messiah will be a bridge to heaven, a preacher of righteousness, a grain of wheat which falls to the ground. Mary knows the prophecies. The long-awaited one will be born of a virgin (Isaiah 7:14).

Mary never expects that virgin will be her.

In ancient culture, a woman's value rests in her virginity. Sexual purity isn't just an ethical burden, but an esteemed badge. A daughter's chastity determines whether a family walks in shame or celebration through the town streets. Luke removes any question about Mary's sexual status by mentioning her virginity not once, but twice. Her honor and her family's honor are intact.

When an angel tells her she will become mysteriously pregnant before the wedding, Mary knows the complications: doubt, discomfort, ridicule, and exile.

Both her current validity and her future vows are on the line.

"How can this be?" she asks.

Perhaps what's most notable isn't what Mary does but what Mary leaves undone.

We don't see her devising her destiny, consulting her calendar, running the numbers in her head. She doesn't try to defend herself or scrap together a new plan.

Instead, she focuses on the *Holy Who* instead of the *everyday what.*

Though circumstances swirl around her, she rises above by focusing on the Almighty God she knows instead of every unknown detail, teaching us:

Shifting your focus from the *everyday what* to the *Holy Who* un-complicates life.

In Him, we find grace. In Him we find peace. In Him, we find joy. In Him, we find simplicity. In Him, we find a way forward and never have to look back.

Reflection Questions:

1. In what area of your life are you more focused on the *everyday what* than the *Holy Who*?
2. What will you do to trust God with every unknown detail?
3. Where are you struggling to find peace with God, with others, or with yourself?
4. What steps do you need to take through prayer or worship to refocus?
5. How will you embrace Advent to find rest for your soul?

DAY SIX
WHEN YOU WONDER WHERE'S GOD
LUKE 1:28 NIV

28 The angel went to her and said, “Greetings, you who are highly favored! The Lord is with you.”

For a moment, imagine yourself a tweenaged girl. Your pulse races. Pupils dilate. Skin turns clammy and sweaty. You gasp to catch your breath. Hair stands on prickly end.

A mighty warrior angel glows before you. He says you’re favored, and the Lord is with you, with you, with you.

Those words echo deep in your soul along with the wonder of the moment. This is the first of many wonders and joys that will come to you. But it’s those first words to which you must cling.

He is with you, with you, with you.

He is with you when your son disappears for days to teach in the temple.
He is with you when you ask for wedding wine and receive a gruff response.
He is with you when you watch your son ridiculed and run out of town.
He is with you when you weep at the feet of His shredded body.

He is with you, with you, with you.

In Immanuel, the words of the angel reach the farthest outposts of humanity. Immanuel means “God with us” and refers to the Christ child. The angel says Mary is “highly favored,” reminding us that not only is God with us, but He has our best interests at heart. He delights in us and loves us. That’s why God with us is such good news.

He is with you, with you, with you.

No matter where you find yourself in life, in relationships, in work, in this holiday season, rest assured, He is with you, with you, with you. And that’s reason to celebrate.

Reflection Questions:

1. What do you imagine it would have been like to be Mary when the angel appeared?
2. How has your life changed because God is with you?
3. In what area of your life do you need to remember God is with you, with you, with you?
4. How will you live your life differently as you more deeply embrace the reality that God is with you?
5. What do you find most encouraging from today’s lesson?

DAY SEVEN
THE ONE THING YOU MUST DO THIS CHRISTMAS
LUKE 1:29 NIV

29 Mary was greatly troubled at his words and wondered what kind of greeting this might be.

The startling sight of a giant, glowing creature sent shivers down Mary's youthful spine. Yet Mary contemplated the angel's every word: "Greetings, you who are highly favored! The Lord is with you" (Luke 1:28).

Mary knew how to savor the signs of the Savior. In Luke 2:19, after the narrator describes the events of that first Christmas morning, he tells us: "Mary treasured up all these things and pondered them in her heart."

Every interaction and encounter—from the leaping in the womb to the bright shining star—tuck in Mary's mind and heart. She doesn't just keep everything safe and sound in her heart's treasure chest, Mary also ponders.

The word *ponder* means "to draw a conclusion by comparing." It's what happens when you look at the parts and put them together to understand the whole. This kind of pondering is like connecting the dots or putting the pieces of the puzzle together so you see the wondrous, glorious God picture. Through pondering, Mary savors each moment.

What does Mary ponder? Gabriel's surprising greeting. Elizabeth's prophetic words. The shepherds' stories. The gifts of the Magi. The prophecies of the Messiah's arrival. Every new word, every new encounter, every new event yields more insight to the unfolding picture.

The one thing you must do this Christmas season: **Savor the signs of the Savior.**

Live eyes wide open to God's presence today. Flip your Bible open and rummage for the syllables the Holy Spirit speaks. Crawl onto your Heavenly Papa's lap through prayer. Ponder and treasure as you celebrate and savor the signs of the Savior. And remember, as you ponder, the Lord is with you.

Reflection Questions:

1. Read Luke 2:51. Why do you think Luke echoes this detail?
2. What spiritual disciplines help you ponder and treasure Christ more?
3. How will you engage in these spiritual disciplines this holiday season?
4. How does savoring the Savior help you grow in prayer, worship, and gratitude?
5. What do you find most challenging in today's devotional? What do you find most comforting?

DAY EIGHT
WHEN HARD THINGS HAPPEN
LUKE 1:30-33 NIV

30 But the angel said to her, "Do not be afraid, Mary; you have found favor with God. 31 You
will conceive and give birth to a son, and you are to call him Jesus. 32 He will be great and
will be called the Son of the Most High. The Lord God will give him the throne of his father
David, 33 and he will reign over Jacob's descendants forever; his kingdom will never end."

When hard things happen, we attempt to race back to normal double-time. We hope God will raise us up to be a stronger, faster, and more effective model for greatness. We'll tell a better story, find a better apartment, snag a better job. We want instant repayment, a restitution to ensure our identities before the world.

But Mary sets aside pretense for providence.

What can she really offer?

Mary does not attempt to spin her appearance, save face, avoid humiliation. She strips herself of everything to be wholly available. She allows God's sufficiency to radiate through her. When it comes to the kingdom of God…

Weak is the new strong.

The apostle Paul echoes this refrain: "Therefore I will boast all the more gladly about my weaknesses, so that Christ's power may rest on me" (2 Corinthians 12:9).

This season allow God's sufficiency to shine through your deficiency.

Reflection Questions:

1. Where do you feel the most weak and deficient right now?
2. What makes it hard for you to believe God will use your weaknesses?
3. How will you make yourself available to God in your weaknesses?
4. Using the Color Method, what stood out to you most from today's Scripture?
5. What do you find most challenging in today's reading? What do you find most comforting?

DAY NINE
WHAT IT REALLY MEANS TO BE HUMAN
LUKE 1:38 NIV

38 "I am the Lord's servant," Mary answered. "May your word to me be fulfilled." Then the angel left her.

On receiving the news she will become impregnated by the power of the Holy Spirit, Mary identifies herself as the Lord's servant. She acknowledges and embraces the deepest truth of what it means to be human—created for God and belonging to Him. Mary shows us:

The best way to receive the full life is to give yourself away.

The word *servant* can be translated *slave*.

The Lord's slave recognizes an exalted status and reveals one who performs humble service with great love and loyalty. This term describes David, Joshua, and Israel. Therefore, Mary represents what God called Israel to become.

In this one statement, Mary sets the world's posture toward service on its head. She isn't searching for autonomy, but a new relationship with God. The angel did not come down and demand obedience with punitive devices. Mary is not repaying a debt, nor has she led a rebellion, nor is she a captured prisoner of war. She doesn't experience the more common avenues of slavery.

Yet she submits herself as a *servant of the Lord, a slave of the Lord* in God's redemptive plan.

Mary gives us a powerful gift this Advent as she embraces the purpose of true humanity. If you want to get a full life, give yourself away.

Reflection Questions:

1. How do you describe your posture toward God this holiday season?
2. In what area of your life do you most need to take on the posture of a servant?
3. Where do you struggle most to live servant-hearted? Why?
4. Where do you find it easy to live servant-hearted? Why?
5. What comfort is possible in being a servant of God daily/weekly/monthly?

DAY TEN
GOD CAN EVEN DO THIS
LUKE 1:39-40 NIV

[39] At that time Mary got ready and hurried to a town in the hill country of Judea, [40] where she entered Zechariah's home and greeted Elizabeth.

Six months into Elizabeth's pregnancy, Mary travels to see her cousin. The story of Elizabeth and Zechariah and the story of Mary and Joseph couldn't be more different.

One couple celebrates decades of marriage. One couple hasn't tied the knot.
One couple tries to have a baby for years. One couple never made a single attempt.
One couple is plunged into silence. One couple is thrust into hiding.
One couple gives birth to a boy who waves people back to God. One couple gives birth to a boy who is God.

Mary doesn't compare her situation to Elizabeth's or vice-versa. They both rejoice for each other's place within God's plan. Through the stories of Zechariah and Elizabeth and Joseph and Mary, we discover the divine principle:

God can multitask.

Maybe you're unskilled at multitasking (like me). Or you're a stellar multitasker. Either way, rest assured: God is better. When God accomplishes one plan, He accomplishes a dozen more.

You may be tempted to think God will work...
in their family *or* yours.
in that person's life *or* yours.
in that ministry *or* yours.

None of these are true because God can multitask.

God never operates from a *this or* mentality. His approach is always *this and.*

What joy and freedom await in trusting that God will accomplish His cosmic goals for the history of the world and His personal goals for you at the same time. God is omniscient and omnipotent—the supreme multitasker. He works in the lives of individuals like you and me (note: not you *or* me). The next time you're tempted to fall into a scarcity mindset, remember that God is so big He can save the world and solve your problems at the same time.

Reflection Questions:

1. How does a scarcity mindset affect your attitudes and actions toward others?
2. Where are you most tempted to believe God will work in one situation *or* another?
3. How does reflecting on God's ability to multitask help you avoid the comparison trap?
4. Describe a time you experienced God working in your life and the life of another at the same time.
5. What do you find most encouraging in today's devotional?

DAY ELEVEN
WHEN SOMEONE PIERCES YOUR HEART
LUKE 1:41-45 NIV

41 When Elizabeth heard Mary's greeting, the baby leaped in her womb, and Elizabeth
was filled with the Holy Spirit. 42 In a loud voice she exclaimed: "Blessed are you among
women, and blessed is the child you will bear! 43 But why am I so favored, that the mother of
my Lord should come to me? 44 As soon as the sound of your greeting reached my ears, the
baby in my womb leaped for joy. 45 Blessed is she who has believed that the Lord would fulfill
his promises to her!"

Mary's visit to Elizabeth isn't just the meeting of two mothers; this is the meeting of two infants. In a booming voice that surprises everyone, Elizabeth proclaims Mary as blessed among women, her child blessed among all infants.

One chapter later, Simon prophesies to Mary, "A sword will pierce your own soul too" (Luke 2:35).

Sometimes it's hard to wrap our minds around the promises and piercings of God. If we're honest...

We want reward without the reckoning.
We want strength without the sacrifice.
We want blessings without the breaking.

Yet our Savior is one who suffers. Jesus invites, "Come and follow me."

Christ waits for you in the promises and the piercings.

Jesus is the Savior who knows the promises and piercings are integral to one another. Death and new life are not opposite ends of a spectrum, but a tension that pulls our lives into dynamic unity with the cross. From the sweet scent of a newborn to the blood and fecal matter running down His pierced body, He knows all the promises and all the piercings—yours too.

Reflection Questions:

1. Are you in a season of promises or piercings right now? Explain.
2. When have you been blindsided by a blessing? Blindsided with brokenness?
3. Read Luke 24:25-26. How was suffering part of Jesus' fulfillment of God's promises?
4. How have you experienced Jesus in both the promises and the piercings?
5. What do you find most challenging in today's devotional?

DAY TWELVE
HOW (NOT) TO BE PULLED APART
MATTHEW 1:18 NASB

18 Now the birth of Jesus Christ was as follows: when His mother Mary had been betrothed to Joseph, before they came together she was found to be with child by the Holy Spirit.

Imagine the joy and delight, the anxiety and fear of Mary. Bolts of emotion thunder through her pregnant body as the impossible becomes possible inside her womb.

Pause for a moment to reflect on your emotions. What are you really feeling today?

Sentimental or stressed?
Festive or frazzled?
Lively or lonely?
Hopeful or hurt?
Wonderful or worried?

No matter what you're feeling, you're not alone in those feelings.

I feel them, too. We all do.

The Christmas season stirs all the feelings, ranging from the sad to the mad to the glad. Yet in the holiday rush, we often stuff those feelings—not just with sugar cookies and eggnog, but with raging busyness and shellacked niceties.

Yet Advent calls us to prepare our hearts for the arrival of a promise, a Savior, a King. Advent asks us to open our hearts and take emotional inventory that we may make room for Him.

The arrival of Christ is a personal story. A story for you and me. One we need to stop and listen to—that's why we need to "pull apart" from all the distraction and noise of the season.

This season you must pull apart so you don't pull apart.

Will you stop right now and ask Christ to be born anew in you?

Ask the Prince of Peace to fill you with holy shalom.

Ask the Light of the World to illuminate your heart.
Ask the Beloved to overwhelm you with His love.
Ask the Wonderful to awaken your sense of holy wonder.

May you not miss this opportunity to pull apart so you are not pulled apart.

Reflection Questions:

1. List five emotions you feel right now.
2. Through prayer, ask God to reveal what's stirring those emotions within you.
3. Which areas do you sense God wants to meet and heal you? Celebrate with you?
4. What steps will you take to pull apart from the busyness this season so you're not pulled apart?
5. Read Psalm 139:2. What comfort do you find in this passage regarding your emotions?

DAY THIRTEEN
WHEN YOU'RE CAUGHT IN THE MIDDLE
MATTHEW 1:22-25 NASB

22 Now all this took place to fulfill what was spoken by the Lord through the
prophet: 23 "Behold, the virgin shall be with child and shall bear a Son, and they shall call
His name Immanuel," which translated means, "God with us." 24 And Joseph awoke from his
sleep and did as the angel of the Lord commanded him, and took Mary as his wife, 25 but kept
her a virgin until she gave birth to a Son; and he called His name Jesus.

Our friend Joseph sits in a pretzel of a predicament.

He thinks he's found the one but soon discovers she's pregnant—and Joseph isn't the father. The promised wife gets pregnant, ruins his reputation, and betrays his heart.

Joseph is just a man, Matthew tells us, a righteous and good and kind man, yet he wakes up to a scandal that will soon become the chatter of the town.

Joseph is caught in a mess he didn't make.

Perhaps that's one reason our friend Matthew pauses as he records Joseph's predicament to tell us that all this mess took place to fulfill what the prophet had spoken. The name that Joseph will give his son means "God with us."

Joseph whispers a sacred yes to God and takes Mary as his wife. Joseph owns the mess by legitimizing it with his own name. But until the child is born, Mary is more a roommate than a wife, and that's messy, too.

Maybe you feel caught in the middle of a mess this Christmas. Family members fighting. Mourning a loss. Missing your loved ones. Feeling forgotten. Staring at an empty crib.

God knows His way through your mess.

Remember that it's in a mess that the Messiah is born—in the life of Joseph and in us. Invite Christ into your place of broken promises, your place of pain today.

No matter what kind of pretzel of a predicament, God knows the way through.

Reflection Questions:

1. If you were God, how would you have come to earth?
2. What do you think were Joseph's biggest worries about Mary?
3. What's your biggest pretzel of a predicament right now?
4. How is God revealing His presence in the middle of your mess?
5. Using the Color Method, what stood out to you most from today's Scripture?

DAY FOURTEEN
ONE QUESTION TO ANSWER THIS CHRISTMAS
MATTHEW 1:19-21 NASB

19 And Joseph her husband, being a righteous man and not wanting to disgrace her,
planned to send her away secretly. 20 But when he had considered this, behold, an angel of
the Lord appeared to him in a dream, saying, "Joseph, son of David, do not be afraid to take
Mary as your wife; for the Child who has been conceived in her is of the Holy Spirit. 21 She will
bear a Son; and you shall call His name Jesus, for He will save His people from their sins."

Joseph enters the first stage of marriage in Jewish culture, a betrothal, then his wife-to-be tells a cockamamie story of becoming pregnant without the involvement of another man.

The whole tale feels like a sham, yet with courage and compassion Joseph decides to hide Mary's indiscretion and send her away. This kindness will save her life because if Joseph races to the courthouse and files for divorce, then Mary will be disowned or, worse, killed.

A divine dream intercepts Joseph's plan. Perhaps we shouldn't be surprised. The son of Jacob, also named Joseph, was known as a dreamer. God has a history of speaking to men named Joe through dreams. This time heaven intercepts this Joseph with a surprise dream that reveals Mary's story isn't cockamamie after all.

Mary has offered a sacred yes—a yes to God—and now Joseph is given the opportunity to give a sacred yes to fathering God's Son. This often overlooked member of God's cast reminds us:

When God calls, there's no better answer than a sacred yes.

In the season of Advent, God longs to hear your sacred yes to His plans, His schedule, His time with you. Will you give a sacred yes to all Christ has planned for you?

Reflection Questions:

1. What do you sense the Holy Spirit nudging you to do that seems like a stretch?
2. Describe a time when you didn't understand God's plan until later.
3. When you look at the remaining days until Christmas, where do you sense God calling you to give a sacred yes?
4. What's something on your calendar you need to say no to in order to give God your sacred yes?
5. Using the Color Method, what stood out to you most from today's Scripture?

DAY FIFTEEN
THE REAL RULES OF CAESAR
LUKE 2:1 KJV

1 And it came to pass in those days, that there went out a decree from Caesar Augustus, that all the world should be taxed.

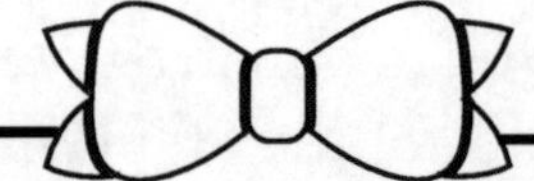

The writer of the Gospel of Luke sets the scene for the birth of Christ by noting that Jesus' birth occurs at a particular time, in a particular place, under a particular system of power.

Sometimes in the rush to embrace the infant, we skip by the significance of Luke's historical context like pebbles across a lake. Yet the writer notes that Caesar Augustus ordered a global decree for taxation. These details add more than a factual framework for the story; they speak of God's rule in a world that appears to be controlled by the Romans.

The grand-nephew of Julius Caesar, Augustus was born Gaius Octavius. The Roman Senate recognized Octavian as the leader of the Roman empire and bestowed on him the title *Augustus*, meaning "exalted one." One ancient inscription described him, "Divine Augustus Caesar, son of god, imperator of land and sea, the benefactor and savior of the whole world." The announcement of the census signaled his universal power that extended to "all the world," and "all went to be taxed" (Luke 2:1, 3).

Those who lived under the Roman Empire were accustomed to being overworked and overtaxed. The financial burden proved so intense that survival required many families to sell their land. In the ancient world, land was considered a family's most precious asset because it had been held by their ancestors for generations. When a family gave up their land, they lost their prized possession and the source of their livelihood.

The setting alerts us that though Augustus may have appeared to be sovereign over the world, God remains the true almighty power. If God used Caesar's harsh decree to move His plan forward, then even the most powerful earthly rulers remain His subjects.

The Roman Empire was used to fulfill the purposes of God.

The most powerful rulers on earth are always subject to the most powerful God.

Reflection Questions:

1. What are three areas of your life where you feel most in control?
2. What prompts a sense of lack of control in your job, home, or everyday life?
3. In what ways will you practice surrendering control?
4. How often have you seen God use something out of your control for your good?
5. What do you find most challenging and comforting in today's devotional?

DAY SIXTEEN
A TALE OF TWO EMPIRES
LUKE 2:2-3 (KJV)

2 And this taxing was first made when Cyrenius was governor of Syria.
3 And all went to be taxed, every one into his own city.

The oppression of the Roman Empire crushes its residents—especially the Israelites—who live at the pleasure of the Emperor. Yet no one dares resist the Empire, because the penalty for insurrection is the Roman cross.

Why is this backdrop so important? Because it provides a sharp contrast between the rule of the Roman Empire and the rule of Christ.

The Roman Empire rules ruthlessly.
Christ serves sacrificially.

The Roman Empire takes and takes.
Christ gives and gives.

The Roman Empire leads by fear and terror.
Christ leads by love and justice.

The Roman Empire grows rich by oppression.
Christ gives up everything to provide freedom.

Christ's arrival not only upends the political landscape, but also upends our heartscape.

Whatever shadow you're living under, Christ wants to set up a new rule and reign in your life today.

Reflection Questions:

1. In addition to the list above, how do earthly rulers differ from Christ's rule?
2. Where do you most you need to make Christ ruler of your life?
3. How is the rule of Christ better than the rule of the earthly rulers to you personally?
4. What needs to be upended most in your heartscape?
5. What do you find most challenging and comforting from today's devotional?

DAY SEVENTEEN

HOW TO FEAST THIS CHRISTMAS

LUKE 2:4-5 KJV

4 Joseph also went up from Galilee, out of the city of Nazareth, into Judea, to the city of
David, which is called Bethlehem, because he was of the house and lineage of David, 5 to be
registered with Mary, his betrothed wife, who was with child.

The journey of Joseph and Mary sounds like an Airbnb travelogue. Yet the significance of this geographic journey cannot be overstated.

Our friend Luke parses his words with great care. In the Old Testament, the phrase "went up" describes travel to Jerusalem. This phrase acknowledges more than a gain in physical elevation; it designates Jerusalem as the city of God.

Yet Joseph travels five miles south of Jerusalem to Bethlehem. In announcing Jesus' birth in Luke 1:32, the angel Gabriel proclaims, "He will be great and will be called the Son of the Most High. The Lord God will give him the throne of his father David." Zechariah echoes this in his song in Luke 1:69.

Why is Luke so concerned with this heritage?

Because for thousands of years the Israelites have been waiting for the Messiah to arrive in the house of David. Like David, Jesus is from Bethlehem (1 Samuel 17:12).

Luke highlights that Jesus fulfills the ancient prophecies and God's plan. Jesus continues God's story of redemption.

Bethlehem means "House of Bread" in Hebrew. Here God bakes the divine recipe:

The Bread of Life rises in the House of Bread.

When the miraculous feeding of thousands echoes God's feeding of the Israelites in the desert, Jesus reveals His identity: "I am the bread of life; he who comes to Me will not hunger" (John 6:35).

If the kingdom of heaven were a loaf of bread, the recipe might include:

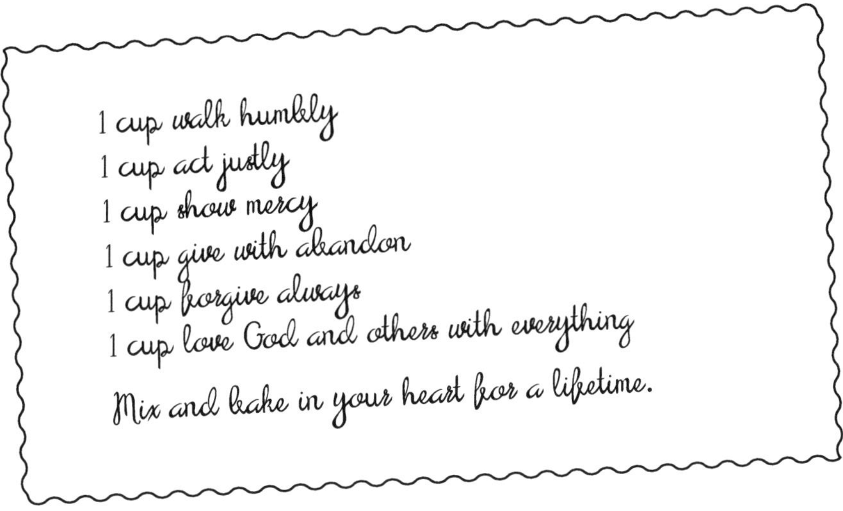

Throughout this holiday season you will be invited to many feasts and celebrations, but only the Bread of Life will bring you joy and satisfy your soul.

Reflection Questions:

1. What are you tempted to satisfy your soul with other than the Bread of Life?
2. In what ways have you been savoring the signs of the Savior?
3. How will you pull away to feast on the Bread of Life this week?
4. Using the Color Method, what stood out to you most from today's reading?
5. What do you think you need to do differently this week to allow the recipe of God's kingdom to rise in your heart?

DAY EIGHTEEN
WHERE REAL POWER REIGNS
LUKE 2:6 NIV

6 While they were there, the time came for the baby to be born.

A paradox offers a seemingly contradictory, but true statement, like the opening of Dickens' novel, *A Tale of Two Cities*: "It was the best of times; it was the worst of times."

Born during the rule of a dictator, Jesus poses a paradox in Himself. The Israelites anticipate a ruler and king as the Messiah.

Yet the Messiah arrives in the basement of a rundown Bethlehem barn.

The Pax Romana, a time of relative calm within the government and military, began during the reign of the first Roman emperor, Caesar Augustus. The Romans kept pax (or peace) through a giant, ruthless army who squashed every hint of rebellion. They used public execution to demonstrate their power. The pax of the Roman Empire came at a dear price for the people forced into it.

The Jews wait for the Messiah to arrive as a military and political leader to overthrow Pax Romana and establish Israel's throne in Jerusalem.

Compared to Caesar Augustus the rex, pontifex, maximus, Jesus shows up as powerless, helpless, weak.

Caesar reigned from a throne while Jesus reigned from hay.

God continues to prove that no matter how developed our theology, God cannot

be contained. From the birth of the Messiah to God's presence in our everyday lives, the Creator continually flips, twists, and jumbles our expectations.

Much like the Israelites, we have our own expectation of how God will arrive in our lives. We pray for healing or restoration or financial stability, but scratch our heads in confusion and disbelief when God doesn't protect, provide, or produce in the ways we predict.

God is a mystery, neither fully understood nor described. Yahweh stoops down from His heavenly throne to wipe our tears, forgive our sins, and dwell among us. God sends Jesus to redeem the world by reigning from a bed of hay, not an earthly throne.

Reflection Questions:

1. Fill in the blank: "If only God __________, then my life would be __________."
2. What are your top three unmet expectations when it comes to God?
3. How has this Advent season served as an opportunity to realign your expectations?
4. On a scale of 1 to 10, how well do you embrace the mystery of God?
5. What steps will you take to leave more room for the mystery of God in your life?

DAY NINTEEN
WHAT TO DO WHEN YOU DON'T FEEL CHRISTMASY
LUKE 2:7 KJV

7 And she brought forth her firstborn son, and wrapped him in swaddling clothes, and laid
him in a manger; because there was no room for them in the inn.

Where was Jesus born?

The Greek word for *inn* can refer to a commercial establishment, but it's unlikely that Bethlehem could sustain such an establishment since this tiny village lacked a major thoroughfare.

This word *inn* also translates "guest room." In ancient Palestine, peasant homes were often built with an upper level dedicated to living space and a lower level for animals.

Joseph and Mary probably anticipated being guests of friends or family, but the census or other circumstances have led to overcrowding. The young couple finds temporary residence in the lower level—among troughs and animal tracks.

You'll note: This more plausible scenario wipes away the tradition of a cruel innkeeper who doesn't love Baby Jesus. While that innkeeper makes for dramatic storytelling, he doesn't appear in the Gospel accounts. And Mary doesn't need any additional drama: the manger provides enough.

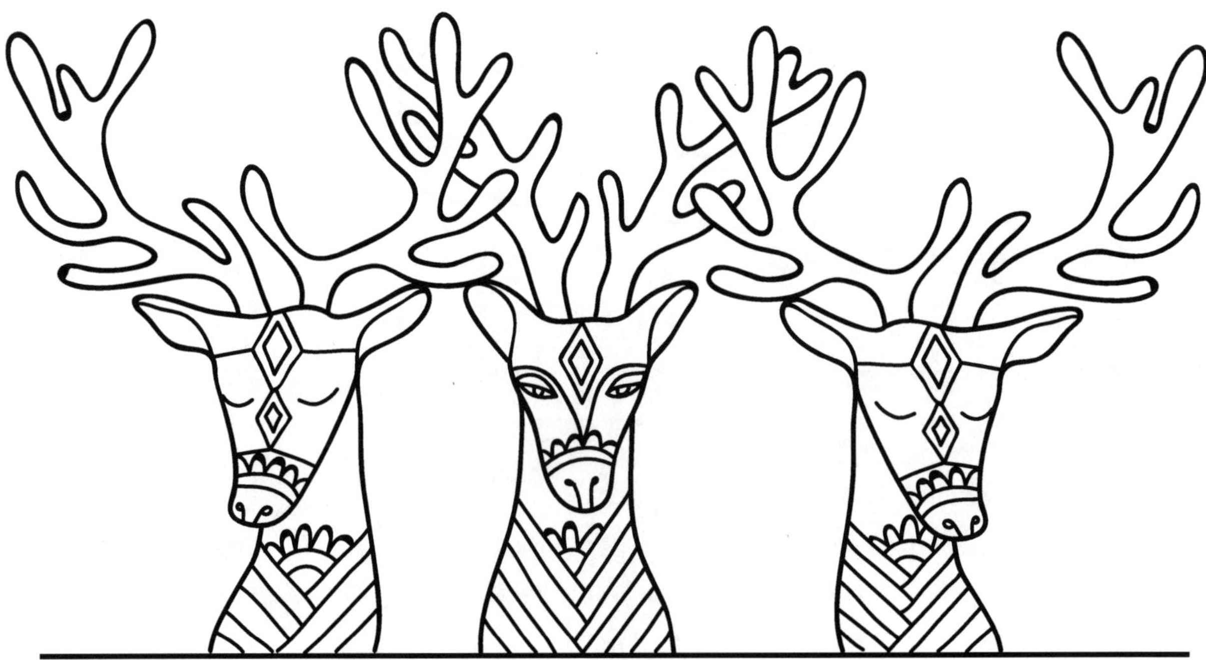

The manger lacks twinkling Christmas lights, favorite carols, and gingerbread cookies. The couple awakens in an unfamiliar, uncomfortable place. Yet within this setting Christ enters our world and everything changes.

God becomes one of us so that we can be one with Him.

> In a manger, our Peace is born.
> In a manger, our Hope is born.
> In a manger, our Strength is born.
> In a manger, our Joy is born.
> In a manger, our Wonder is born.

If you're struggling to lasso your inner Grinch or not feeling Christmasy this year, perhaps it's time to make Him room and allow the work of God to be born in you.

Reflection Questions:

1. What does Christmas mean to you?
2. What do you think Christmas means to God?
3. How do you imagine heaven celebrates Christmas?
4. What's most meaningful to you about Jesus being born in a manger?
5. Read Galatians 5:22-23. What fruit of the Spirit do you most need born in you this Christmas season?

DAY TWENTY
WHERE GOD PERFORMS HIS GREATEST WORKS
LUKE 2:8-12 NIV

[8] And there were shepherds living out in the fields nearby, keeping watch over their flocks at
night. [9] An angel of the Lord appeared to them, and the glory of the Lord shone around them,
and they were terrified.

[10] But the angel said to them, "Do not be afraid. I bring you good news that will cause great
joy for all the people. [11] Today in the town of David a Savior has been born to you; he is the
Messiah, the Lord. [12] This will be a sign to you: You will find a baby wrapped in cloths and
lying in a manger."

If God does something big, then how does God get the word out? If you were on God's publicity team, what would you recommend for announcing big news?

You might host a press conference at the Temple Mount in Jerusalem with all the movers and shakers of society present—people of means, people of influence—such as key religious leaders or even Caesar Augustus. Imagine the headlines: There's A New King in Town.

Yet God handpicked shepherds. Those who cared for sheep occupied a class near the bottom of society. Within a family or community, those assigned to take care of the sheep were primarily children, elderly, and women—people unable to fulfill more important communal tasks.

Over the years, shepherds became viewed with contempt and distrust. Since they spent so much time alone searching for pasture for their animals, they were sometimes seen as socially awkward and disconnected.

Yet God entrusts the greatest news of all time to shepherds. Ten thousand angels stand at rapt attention waiting to deliver world-changing news to peasants not princes. Perhaps we shouldn't be surprised.

The Word performs His greatest works among the lowly.

What's the importance of this proclamation to the shepherds? God's PR campaign to the marginalized reminds us that no one ranks better than anyone else.

Jesus came to end division, to end demarcation, to end stereotypes, to end the ugly whispers of *us versus them* and *those people*.

Christ's arrival invites us to open our hearts and hands and tables wider than they've ever been before. And see the glory of the Lord shining in each human, all created in the image of God.

Reflection Questions:

1. If Jesus were born today, to whom do you think the angels would make their announcement?
2. In what ways is God calling you to reach out to the young, the weak, the old, and the outcast?
3. What steps will you take to defend the defenseless and speak up for those who have no voice?
4. What changes in your attitude and actions do you need to make toward the marginalized?
5. Using the Color Method, what stood out to you most from today's reading?

DAY TWENTY ONE
THE SONG YOU'RE CREATED TO SING
LUKE 2:13-14 NIV

13 Suddenly a great company of the heavenly host appeared with the angel, praising God and
saying, 14 "Glory to God in the highest heaven, and on earth peace to those on whom his favor
rests."

On a star-studded night, God slashes open the veil of heaven like silver wrapping paper to reveal a host of angels.

Is this gift for the shepherds? For us? For God's delight? Or perhaps all?

Their radiance fills the sky like a collection of rare jewels. Their voices harmonize in holy unison. They repeat the refrain that's as old as the Father of Time.

"Glory to God," they sing, the words emanating from the hollows and the hallows of their innermost beings.

Don't mistake this celestial gathering as a sparse collection of angels or a quartet of cherubs. A heavenly host is a mighty army. This host of angels isn't declaring war; they're proclaiming peace.

After all, the Prince of Peace has come.

"Glory to God," they sing.

Look closely at the words of the angels.

"Glory to God in the highest heaven, and on earth peace to those on whom his favor rests" (Luke 2:14).

Every word glorifies Him.
Every syllable focuses on Him.
Every praise exalts Him.

"Glory to God," they sing.

If you close your eyes tight enough, pray hard enough, and imagine big enough, you almost hear their song:

"Glory to God, Glory to God, Glory to God."

Like the angels, you are created for worship from the hollows turned hallows of your innermost being.

Worship makes a heart joyful and a joy-filled heart.

Will you dare join the angels chorus right now? Go ahead. Sing aloud: "Glory to God, Glory to God, Glory to God. Glory to God in the highest heaven, and on earth peace to those on whom his favor rests."

Reflection Questions:

1. Where are you tempted to live more for the glory of self than the glory of God?
2. What are three things you will give God glory and praise for right now?
3. Pause to sing Luke 2:14 aloud to God.
4. Using the Color Method, what stood out to you most from today's reading?
5. What do you find most challenging about including your voice in the angels' chorus?

DAY TWENTY TWO
WHEN EVERYTHING GOES WRONG
MATTHEW 2:1-3 HCSB

1 After Jesus was born in Bethlehem of Judea in the days of King Herod, wise men from the
east arrived unexpectedly in Jerusalem, 2 saying, "Where is He who has been born King of
the Jews? For we saw His star in the east and have come to worship Him." 3 When King Herod
heard this, he was deeply disturbed, and all Jerusalem with him.

If you lived in Mary's day among the Jews, you would know Herod the Great was not that great, and you'd long to see him toppled from his overblown throne.

Herod rose to power through political savvy and ruthless violence. After winning the favor of the Roman emperor, he seized Jerusalem from the Parthians in 37 BC, claiming the title "King of the Jews."

What Herod conquered with brute force, he defended with similar brutality. Everyone who resisted Herod was slaughtered. He executed over half the Sanhedrin—the ruling religious class—because they resisted his leadership.

Herod appointed his brother-in-law high priest. When his brother-in-law grew popular with the people, Herod felt threatened. His brother-in-law soon perished in a drowning accident in a super shallow pool.

Herod enjoyed multiple wives but adored Mariamne above the rest. Herod loved her so much that before leaving for a trip to Rome, he instructed his guards that if he died on the journey, they must kill her, so no one else could have her.

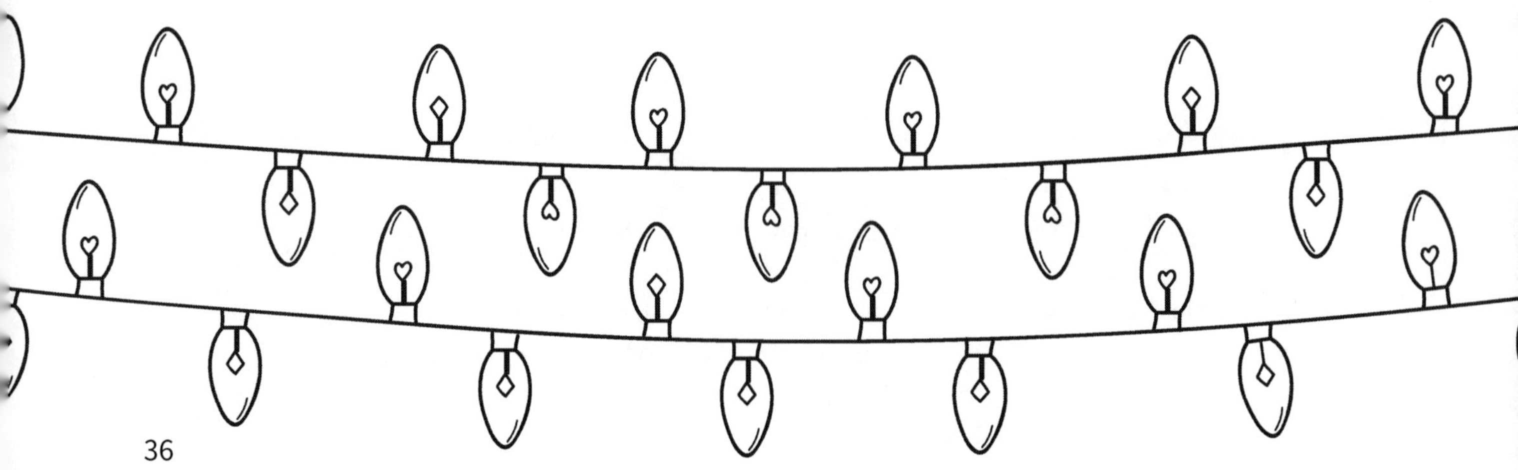

Upon his return, Herod's mother persuaded him that Mariamne was unfaithful, so he murdered her. Mariamne's mother was devastated by Herod's harsh response, so he murdered her, too.

Countless members of the royal family were tortured and executed, including two of his sons, who pleaded for their lives to no avail.

Herod became more insecure as he aged. When he received a visit from dignitaries from the east who sought to honor a new King of the Jews, he hatched a plan to destroy the infant. Unable to find the Bethlehem baby, he issued a decree to kill every boy in Bethlehem and the surrounding vicinity two years old or younger.

Yet even a cruel dictator could not crush the coming Messiah.

Hell's fury is no match for God's faithfulness.

No matter the impossible situation or brutal suffering, remember that even if you lose sight of God, God never loses sight of you. God remains your constant companion.

Reflection Questions:

1. Who is a Herod in your life right now?
2. What aspects of this person make them so hard to love?
3. Which of the person's unhealthy tendencies do you see in yourself?
4. Say a prayer of forgiveness and blessing toward the person. Ask God to work a miracle of transformation in the person's life and your life.
5. Read Ephesians 6:10-20. Which part of the armor of God do you most need as you navigate the Herods in your life?

DAY TWENTY THREE

HOW TO FIND THE LIGHT YOU NEED

MATTHEW 2:9-10 NASB

9 After hearing the king, they [the Magi] went their way; and the star, which they had seen
in the east, went on before them until it came and stood over the place where the Child
was. 10 When they saw the star, they rejoiced exceedingly with great joy.

Have you ever tried to count the stars on a crisp, clear, winter night?

One... two... three... four... sixteen... twenty-five... one-hundred-and... soon trail off.

Scientists, armed with giant telescopes, count and count and continue to count. They say if you take the 10 trillion galaxies of the universe and multiply them by the Milky Way's estimated 100 billion stars, you end up with what looks like a bazillion to this non-scientist... a one followed by two dozen zeros. Sketch the number in the margins, if you like, to glimpse this mind-bender.

Where did all those stars come from?

I love the image of God exhaling stars during the dawn of creation. The Psalmist tells us, "He breathed the word and all the stars were born" (Psalm 33:6 NLT).

God trimmed the night's sky in a twinkling garland of light.

Our friend Matthew tells us that before Jesus' birth, one star stood above them all.

A star breathed by God, handcrafted by God, handpicked by God.

The star shines a guiding light to the Magi, who need to find a needle in a haystack, an infant in hay in an overcrowded town. God burns one star extra bright so the Magi find their way.

You may be tempted to think God only provides signal flares for the Magi, but time and time again throughout the Scripture, we discover this joy:

God knows His way around the dark.

When you find yourself in the inky blackness, unsure of which way to go, look to Christ as your guiding star. Draw close to the Light of the World. In Him, you will find your joy. The Light of the World has come so that you don't have to walk alone in the dark anymore.

Reflection Questions:

1. Which night this week will you step outside to admire God's handiwork in the night sky?
2. In what area of your life do you feel like you're lost or living in the dark?
3. Where do need to hear God say, "This is the way. Walk in it."
4. Using the Color Method, what stood out to you most from today's reading?
5. What do you find most comforting about the enormity of God's creation?

DAY TWENTY FOUR

THIS IS YOUR GREATEST GIFT

MATTHEW 2:11 NASB

11 After coming into the house they saw the Child with Mary His mother; and they fell to the ground and worshiped Him. Then, opening their treasures, they presented to Him gifts of gold, frankincense, and myrrh.

Confession: I often get wrapped up in purchasing the perfect gift for someone. Instead of buying another item that gets stuffed in the back of the closet or donated during spring cleaning, I try to select a memorable, meaningful gift. Yet many times, I don't succeed.

The size doesn't fit. The color appears off. The person already owns three.

These difficulties compound when you shop for The-Person-Who-Has-Everything. You probably have these people in your life. Just when you think you've found the perfect gift, you discover they already own one.

The Bible tells us of gift-givers who face such a challenge with Jesus. Traveling almost 1,000 miles from the east, a group of wise men along with attendants and guards follow a star in anticipation of worshiping the Messiah—the promised King of the Jews.

King Herod stops them in their tracks on their journey. Herod's jaw tightens when he hears of a new king's birth. He plots to murder the child.

When the Magi arrive in Bethlehem, they kneel at Jesus' tiny toes and unwrap treasures for the newborn. Now the presentation of gifts to royalty was a common custom, but consider the selection.

Gold, a precious metal in Scripture, used much like today; frankincense, used as perfume and incense for the altar; and myrrh, a perfume or tonic used when preparing a corpse for burial.

Gold, frankincense, and myrrh demonstrate great reverence and generosity to Jesus, but giving anything to the Savior of the world and Son of God seems downright silly. For Yahweh, who ultimately has everything and is everything, what's an appropriate gift?

The Magi purchase the best gifts—presents of high value—and those gifts support Joseph and Mary when they must flee the country on short notice. But these are not the Magi's greatest gifts. Their greatest offering to Jesus is the gift of themselves, their presence, their full attention.

Jesus doesn't desire your *presents* as much as your *presence*.

As you countdown to Christmas, remember the greatest gift you will give is yourself. Don't forget to carve out time to offer yourself as a gift to the King.

Reflection Questions:

1. How can you give your best present of presence to Jesus on Christmas Day?
2. What do you want most from Jesus this Christmas?
3. When will you create a space for you and those you love to worship, pray, and reflect together on Christmas Eve or Christmas Day?
4. What do you find most challenging this time of year when it comes to being present with others and God?
5. Using the Color Method, what stood out to you most from today's Scripture?

DAY TWENTY FIVE
THE SECRET OF WAITING ON GOD
LUKE 2:36-38 NIV

36 There was also a prophet, Anna, the daughter of Penuel, of the tribe of Asher. She was very
old; she had lived with her husband seven years after her marriage, 37 and then was a widow
until she was eighty-four. She never left the temple but worshiped night and day, fasting and
praying. 38 Coming up to them at that very moment, she gave thanks to God and spoke about
the child to all who were looking forward to the redemption of Jerusalem.

Waiting has never been a popular activity. Perhaps that's why we share a tendency to avoid waiting at all costs.

I crane my neck to count the number of people in line ahead of me.
I check my phone every few minutes for a response.
I refresh the webpage in hopes of an update.

These are among our everyday waits.

Waiting for a diploma. Waiting for a spouse. Waiting for a child. Waiting for a job. Waiting for a promotion. Waiting for retirement.

These are some of our lifelong waits.

Waiting to outgrow insecurities. Waiting for the anxiety to leave. Waiting for the aftershocks of the trauma to end. Waiting for the broken heart to heal. Waiting for the addiction to lose its grip. Waiting for the prodigal to return home.

These are among our heart waits.

Waiting for that sense of God's nearness. Waiting for the word from God that will change everything. Waiting for God to fulfill His promise.

These are among our God waits.

Perhaps we should not be surprised that all the men and women who appear in the opening pages of Luke engage in the spiritual discipline of waiting.

Zechariah. Elizabeth. Mary. Simeon. Anna.

Those who wait for something good, something divine.

Not all who live in Israel wait. Some give up hope. Others stop looking for their rescue and fall into criticism and cynicism.

Zechariah, Elizabeth, Mary, Simeon, and Anna demonstrate that no matter how long the wait, we can remain attentive, hopeful, expectant. As the celebration of Christmas reminds us:

Those who wait on the Lord will be rewarded.

With the arrival of Christmas, I hope and pray your wait will be rewarded with the celebration, wonder, and joy found in Christ.

Reflection Questions:

1. What's your biggest challenge when you wait on God?
2. What inspires and encourages you most about Anna's story?
3. Where are you most likely to give up hope right now?
4. How are you becoming more attentive to God during your wait?
5. Using the Color Method, what stood out to you most from today's devotion?

Made in the USA
Middletown, DE
05 November 2024